32 Arrangements of Favorite Masterpieces

Selections from The Brandenburg Concertos, Eine kleine Nachtmusik, The Four Seasons and more
Arranged for Intermediate Piano by Fred Kern

Alfred's Classic Editions

Copyright © MMVIII by Alfred Publishing Co., Inc.
All Rights Reserved. Printed in USA.
ISBN-10: 0-7390-5745-6
ISBN-13: 978-0-7390-5745-2

Table of Contents

Foreword

Brandenburg Notebook

The six *Brandenburg Concertos* are among the most popular orchestral music of all time. The many familiar themes reveal a wealth of inventive counterpoint, energetic rhythm and varied instrumental color. J. S. Bach (1685–1750) was known as a prolific arranger and, like other composers of his day, he often borrowed from his own works and those of others. Re-arrangements and transcriptions were often formulated to meet a utilitarian need in teaching, performing or concert preparation.

These piano solo arrangements of *Brandenburg* themes will find a useful place for students between the *Notebook for Anna Magdalena Bach* and the more difficult *Two-Part Inventions*. Dynamics in Bach's solo keyboard works were left to the player's discretion except for a few rare instances of registration indications. In these *Brandenburg* selections for piano, it is appropriate to use both gradual and terraced dynamics. However, the player is warned against excessive uses that would be un-stylistic. The ornamentions, as indicated in parentheses, are optional and may be left out entirely or realized as ability permits. A suggested realization of moderate difficulty is notated throughout these selections.

Themes from Water Music

Water Music by George Frederic Handel (1685–1759) is among the most popular instrumental works from the Baroque period. Originally written as a suite for wind instruments, it was intended for outdoor performance and may have been commissioned by King George I to accompany royal boating parties on the Thames. The exact date of composition is not certain, but it is thought to be 1717.

Handel was a very cosmopolitan figure in the musical world of Europe in that he was born in Germany, traveled in Italy and lived nearly 50 years in England. Although his reputation was made primarily as a composer of operas and oratorios, he also composed a large number of masterful instrumental works. Handel was equally famous as an extraordinary performer at the keyboard, particularly for his improvising at the organ and harpsichord.

During the eighteenth-century it was quite common for musicians to be employed by the courts, and they were required to provide not only all of the music for royal events but were also expected to give music instruction to the children of the royal family. Handel's most important contribution to instrumental keyboard music is in the suites and it is thought that the earliest of these was composed for the instruction of Princess Anne, one of his pupils in the court.

Teachers and students today will find these piano solo arrangements from the *Water Music* Suite to be useful in bridging the gap between the few easy dance pieces of Handel and the more difficult suites. In addition to providing some arrangements of his most attractive music, these Handel selections offer a fresh alternative to some other Baroque pieces that have become overly familiar. As was typical in the original manuscripts of the period, dynamics in these pages have been left to the player's discretion. Ornamentation has not been indicated generally, although the performer may feel free to add embellishments when appropriate and as ability permits.

Themes from "Polovtsian Dances" from the Opera *Prince Igor*
Alexander Borodin (1833–1887) has been called the most inspired melodist of the "Russian Five" (including Cui, Balakirev, Mussorgsky, and Rimsky-Korsakov) in spite of the fact that he called himself a "Sunday composer." A chemist by profession, Borodin had an excellent education as a child and learned to play piano and flute. His interests in music continued throughout his life and under the influence of Balakirev he became a nationalistic composer, utilizing Russian and Oriental folkloristic idioms.

His major compositions include symphonies, string quartets, a symphonic sketch and the four-act opera *Prince Igor*. The familiar "Polovtsian Dances" occur within Act II of the opera. They are characterized by their chromatic harmonies, bright colors, graceful melodies and a subtle, exotic and Oriental flavor. Although the opera was unfinished at the time of Borodin's death, the orchestration and incomplete parts were filled in by Rimsky-Korsakov and Glazunov, with the first performance taking place in 1890.

The opera's plot is based on a medieval chronicle, *The Epic of the Army of Igor*, which deals with the campaign against the invading Polovtski, a nomadic tribe inhabiting the steppes of far eastern Russia. In Act II a festival of exotic songs and dances is devised for the entertainment of Prince Igor, who is being held captive in the Polovtski camp. It is from this section of music that the present arrangements for piano were selected.

The "Polovtsian Dances" are best known in their orchestral settings, having been first singled out for concert performance by Rimsky-Korsakov. In addition, they have been a part of the repertoire of Ballet Russe. Most famous among the beloved melodies from Borodin is the one adapted for use in the musical *Kismet* and widely known as "Stranger in Paradise."

Albinoni for Piano
Tomaso Albinoni (1671–1751), a versatile composer and an expert violinist, was born in Venice, Italy, and made important contributions to the music of the Italian Baroque. Although he was a prolific opera composer (at times writing as many as five per year), very little of these works survive. He is known today as a composer of symphonies, trio sonatas and violin sonatas. One of his major contributions to orchestral literature is in the form of the instrumental concerto. Albinoni's writing differentiated clearly between the orchestra and the solo instrument, with the contrasts between the *tutti* and the *solo* being distinct and well-defined.

Albinoni's works were known and admired by J.S. Bach, as evidenced by Bach's occasional use of Albinoni themes as fugue subjects and the fact that he gave his students figured basses of Albinoni works as exercises. In addition to Bach, Albinoni's famous contemporaries were Torelli, Corelli and Vivaldi.

Throughout the history of music composition, composers have "recycled" melodies, themes and ideas from their own works and from the works of other composers. Many times this kind of musical "borrowing" is considered the highest form of flattery. Some musicians even went so far as to transcribe entire works of other composers, arranging the music for a different combination of instruments to meet a utilitarian need in teaching or performing. This type of musical activity was considered standard practice, especially acceptable during the Baroque period. The three movements selected and grouped in this arrangement are all examples of the practice of musical borrowing, arranging and re-arranging.

The first movement, "Allegro," was originally written by Albinoni as part of his *Concerto in D,* Op. 7, No. 8, for two oboes and string orchestra. The music around measures 9 and 17 is an example of the *solo* and *tutti* contrasts mentioned previously. It is suggested that performers try to imagine the sounds produced by the two oboes in conversation with the string orchestra and then attempt to project similar contrasts when playing the same music on a piano.

The second movement in this set, "Adagio in G Minor," has come to be known as "the Albinoni Adagio," a favorite of today's listeners and performers. Its appeal is similar to that of Pachelbel's "Canon," or Bach's "Air" from the *Orchestral Suite*, No. 3. This "Adagio" is undoubtedly Albinoni's "greatest hit," although its true origin is not completely clear. Some sources identify it as a movement of a trio sonata for strings and continuo, while others catalogue it as an independent piece for organ and strings.

The last movement selected for this set is another "Allegro," originally written as the opening movement of *Concerto in D,* Op. 7, No. 6, for oboe solo and string orchestra.

Piano students are often encouraged to think "orchestrally" as they try for expanded tonal variety on an acoustic piano. This type of aural imagining can be nurtured in a very concrete way with today's electronic sound samplers and sequencers. Teachers might assign students to re-arrange, or reconstruct, these Albinoni arrangements by using the original instrumentation as a guide.

Eine kleine Nachtmusik
Wolfgang Amadeus Mozart's (1756–1791) serenade for strings, *Eine kleine Nachtmusik,* K. 525, is an example of his most popular classical style, full of charm and elegance. During the classical period, a suite of more than four movements for chamber ensemble was commonly called a *divertimento* or *serenade.* This work was written in 1787 and originally contained five movements, of which the following four are played today: "Allegro," "Romanze," "Minuet and Trio," and "Rondo."

It is not known the exact occasion for which *Eine kleine Nachtmusik* was composed, but serenades were often written for garden parties, weddings, birthdays, or home concerts for friends or patrons. The title, *Eine kleine Nachtmusik,* means "A Little Night Music," perhaps implying that it was intended for use in a more relaxed setting rather than in a formal concert.

These piano solo arrangements of *Eine kleine Nachtmusik* themes will find a useful place for students between the minuets and allegros of the elementary level and the requirements of the advanced Mozart repertoire. More specifically, these themes can help bridge the gap between the demands of the *Notebook for Nannerl,* the *Wolfgang Notebook,* or the *London Notebook,* the *Fantasy in D Minor,* or any of the nineteen sonatas.

During part of Mozart's life he was a freelance musician. His ability to appeal to the popular taste is revealed in the delicacy and simplicity of this, his most familiar serenade.

The Four Seasons

The Four Seasons ("*Le Quattro Stagioni*") is the original title given to the first four violin concertos of Op. 8 by Antonio Vivaldi (ca. 1678–1741). Published in 1724, these four works are an early example of program music with the score of each concerto being preceded by a descriptive sonnet.

For many years Vivaldi was a director of music at the Pietà Conservatory in Venice where he composed for the excellent student orchestra at the school. He enjoyed great fame during his lifetime and is known to have had significant influence on the music of his contemporaries, including J. S. Bach. In fact, Bach copied and transcribed at least nine of Vivaldi's concertos: six for harpsichord, two for organ and one for four harpsichords and string orchestra (originally for four violins).

The Four Seasons is one of the world's most popular works of concert music. It is often heard in its original form on the programs of major symphony orchestras, as well as in transcription for other instrumental ensembles, such as brass choir.

The themes presented in this collection include some of the most popular melodies from the complete work. Themes have been taken from the first movements of "Spring," "Summer" and "Autumn" and from the second movement of "Winter." The arrangements are presented in the original order, however they may be re-arranged or played separately. Since the four movements cover a range of musical and technical difficulties, teachers may wish to assign them to four different students for performance in recital or repertoire classes. Additionally, teachers will find the suite useful as repertoire which is similar in style and leveling as the selections from Bach's *Notebook for Anna Magdalena Bach.*

Suite of Themes from *The Four Seasons*
I. "Theme from Spring" is one of the most popular melodies from the original work by Vivaldi. It is marked *allegro* and has broken octaves in the accompaniment, reminiscent of Bach's *Musette in D Major.* The mood is lively and spirited and should be played with special attention to the terraced dynamics, which are so typical of the period.

II. "Theme from Summer" is in 3/8 meter and is marked *allegro con molto.* The texture is thin and a feeling of movement must be sustained throughout, in spite of frequent rests in both hands and phrases of varied note-groupings. The overall effect is slow and sustained (the feeling of a hot summer night) although the tempo marking is 100 to the eighth-note.

III. "Theme from Autumn" is in the style of a march with textures of two and three voices. This section provides greater contrast in keyboard color by varying the dynamics and octaves within which the sequential sections imitate the main theme.

IV. "Theme from Winter" is taken from the second movement of the original concerto. The lyrical melody appears over a rapid staccato accompaniment of broken chords and Alberti bass, giving the feeling of a much faster tempo than the *largo* marking might otherwise indicate. The left hand must be kept very light and detached, as heard in a pizzicato string part, while the long melody line is played *cantabile* and sustained.

Selections from
Brandenburg Concerto No. 1

Johann Sebastian Bach
Arranged by Fred Kern

I. ALLEGRO

*realization for ornament below

III. ALLEGRO

IV. MENUETTO

Selections from
Brandenburg Concerto No. 2

Johann Sebastian Bach
Arranged by Fred Kern

I. ALLEGRO

II. ANDANTE

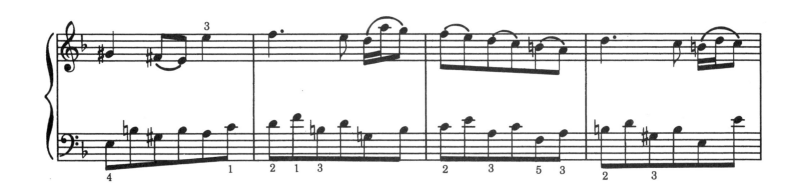

III. ALLEGRO ASSAI

Selection from
Brandenburg Concerto No. 3

Johann Sebastian Bach
Arranged by Fred Kern

I. ALLEGRO

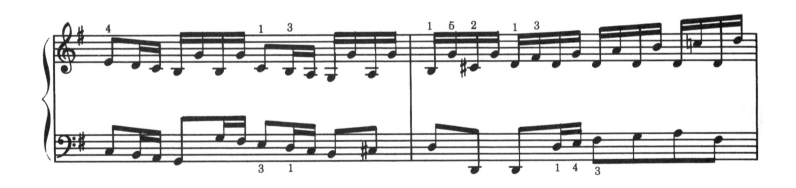

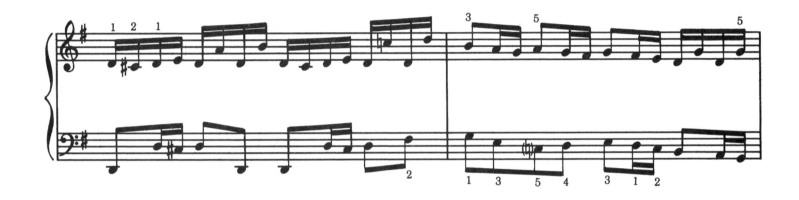

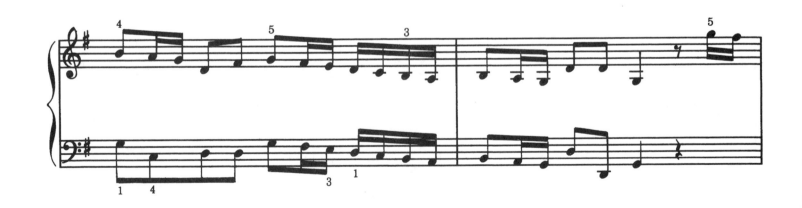

Selections from
Brandenburg Concerto No. 4

Johann Sebastian Bach
Arranged by Fred Kern

I. ALLEGRO

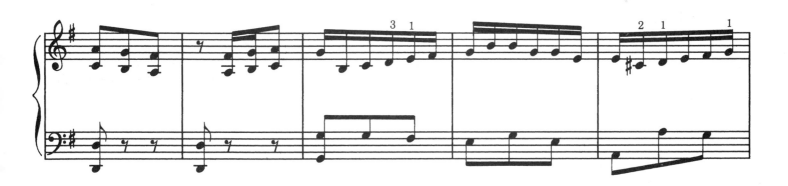

II. ANDANTE

III. PRESTO

Selections from
Brandenburg Concerto No. 5

Johann Sebastian Bach
Arranged by Fred Kern

I. ALLEGRO

III. ALLEGRO*

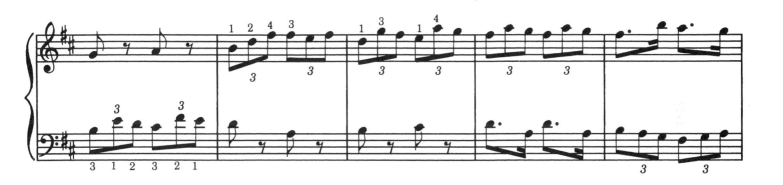

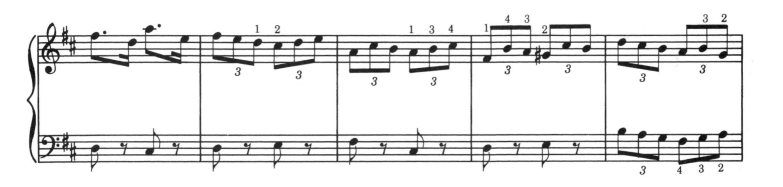

*may also be played in 6/8 time (♩. ♪♫ = ♪ ♪ ♩ ♪)

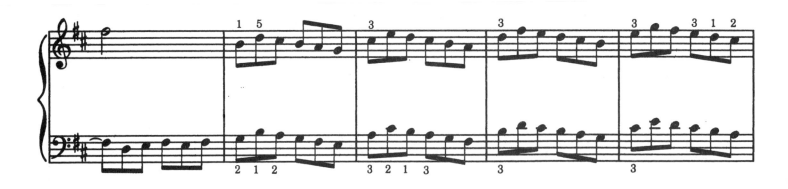

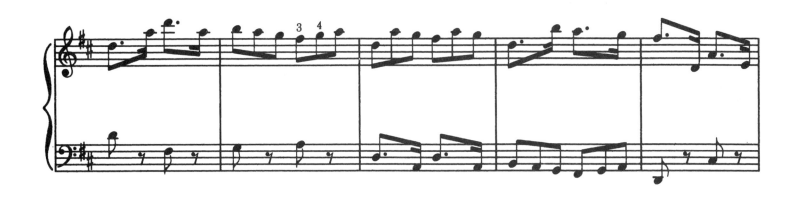

Selections from
Brandenburg Concerto No. 6

Johann Sebastian Bach
Arranged by Fred Kern

III. ALLEGRO

Themes from Water Music

George Frederic Handel
Arranged by Fred Kern

I. Bourrée

simile detached

II. Air

III. Hornpipe*

Allegro ♩ = 144-170

* original: 3/2 meter

IV. Andante

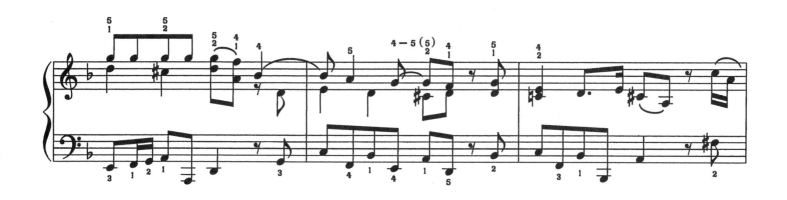

V. Finale

Themes from "Polovtsian Dances"
from the Opera Prince Igor

Alexander Porfirievich Borodin
Arranged by Fred Kern

I. The Polovtsy Maidens

II. Dance of the Polovtsy Maidens

III. Flowing Dance of the Women
Dance of the Wild Men

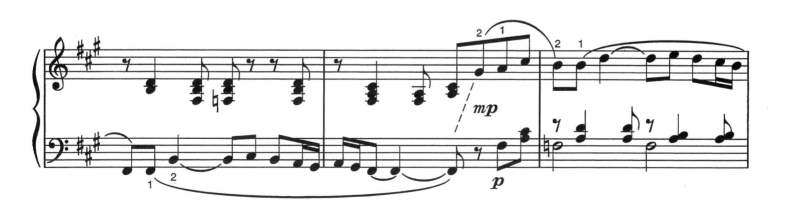

Albinoni for Piano

Tomaso Albinoni
Arranged by Fred Kern

ALLEGRO

from *Concerto in D, Op. 7, No. 8*
for two oboes and string orchestra

ADAGIO

("the Albinoni Adagio")
origin unknown

ALLEGRO

from *Concerto in D, Op. 7, No. 6*
for oboe solo and string orchestra

Eine kleine Nachtmusik

Wolfgang Amadeus Mozart
Arranged by Fred Kern

ALLEGRO

ROMANZE

MENUETTO

RONDO

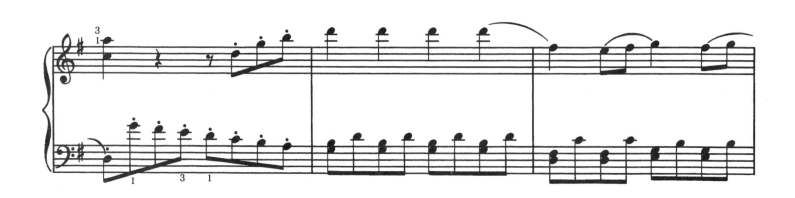

(RH crosses over LH)

The Four Seasons
"Le Quattro Stagioni"

Antonio Vivaldi
Arranged by Fred Kern

Theme from "Spring" Op. 8, No. 1
Movt. I

Theme from "Summer" Op. 8, No. 2

Movt. I

Theme from "Autumn" Op. 8, No. 3

Movt. I

Theme from "Winter" Op. 8, No. 4

Movt. II